pilgrim

THE CREEDS
A COURSE FOR THE CHRISTIAN JOURNEY

Church Publishing
NEW YORK

Authors and Contributors

Authors

Stephen Cottrell is the Bishop of Chelmsford
Steven Croft is the Bishop of Sheffield
Paula Gooder is a leading New Testament writer and lecturer
Robert Atwell is the Bishop of Exeter
Sharon Ely Pearson is a Christian educator in The Episcopal Church

Contributors

Mary Gregory is a priest and Dean of Women's Ministry in the Diocese
of Sheffield
Martyn Snow is the Bishop of Tewkesbury
Graham Tomlin is Dean of St. Mellitus College
Jane Williams teaches Christian doctrine at St. Mellitus College and is
a visiting lecturer in theology at King's College London

pilgrim

THE CREEDS
A COURSE FOR THE CHRISTIAN JOURNEY

STEPHEN COTTRELL
STEVEN CROFT
PAULA GOODER
ROBERT ATWELL
SHARON ELY PEARSON

Contributions from
MARY GREGORY   MARTYN SNOW
GRAHAM TOMLIN   JANE WILLIAMS

Church Publishing
NEW YORK

Copyright © 2014, 2016 Stephen Cottrell, Steven Croft, Robert Atwell
and Paula Gooder

Cover image—Sunset Stairs: John Wollwerth/Shutterstock.com
Under license from Shutterstock.com

ISBN-13: 978-0-89869-956-2 (pbk.)
ISBN-13: 978-0-89869-957-9 (ebook)

First published in the United Kingdom in 2014 by

Church House Publishing
Church House
Great Smith Street
London SW1P 3AZ

First published in the United States in 2016 by

Church Publishing, Incorporated.
19 East 34th Street
New York, New York 10016
www.churchpublishing.org

Scripture quotations from The New Revised Standard Version of the
Bible, copyright 1989 by the Division of Christian Education of the
National Council of the Churches in the USA. Used by permission. All
rights reserved.

Material from *Common Worship: Services and Prayers for the Church of
England* including the Psalter is copyright © The Archbishops' Council
2000–2008 and is used with permission.

Cover and contents design by David McNeill, Revo Design.

Library of Congress Cataloging-in-Publication data

A record of this book is available from the Library of Congress.

Printed in the United States of America

CONTENTS

WELCOME TO *PILGRIM*

Welcome to this course of exploration into the truth of the Christian faith as it has been revealed in Jesus Christ and lived out in the Church down through the centuries.

The aim of this course is to help people explore what it means to be disciples of Jesus Christ. From the very beginning of his ministry, Jesus called people to follow him and become his disciples. The first disciples were called to be with Jesus and to be sent out (Mark 3:14). The Church in every generation shares in the task of helping others hear Christ's call to follow him and to live in his service.

The *Pilgrim* material consists of two groups of four short courses. The **Follow** stage is designed for those who are beginning to explore the faith and what following Jesus will mean. It focuses on four great texts that have been particularly significant to Christian people from the earliest days of the Church:

● The Baptismal Covenant (drawn from the Creeds)

● The Lord's Prayer

● The Beatitudes

● The Commandments

The Follow stage is a beginning in the Christian journey. There is much still to be learned. The four courses in the **Grow** stage—of which this is one—aim to take you further and deeper, building on the Follow stage. They focus on:

● The Creeds

● The Eucharist (and the whole life of prayer and worship)

● The Bible

● The Church and the kingdom (living your whole life as a disciple)

We hope that, in the Grow stage, people will learn the essentials for a life of discipleship. We hope that you will do this in the company of a small group of fellow travelers: people like you who want to find out more about the Christian faith and are considering its claims and challenges.

The material in the Grow stage can also be used by people who have been Christians for many years (like The Bible) as a way of deepening their discipleship.

We have designed the material in the Grow stage so that it can be led by the members of the group: you don't need an expert or a teacher to guide you through. *Pilgrim* aims to help you learn by encouraging you to practice the ancient disciplines of biblical reflection and prayer, which have always been at the heart of the living out of Christian faith.

The format is similar to the Follow stage. Each book has six sessions and, in each session, you will find:

● a **theme**

● some **opening prayers**

● a **"conversation-starter"**

● an opportunity to reflect on a **reading** from Scripture (the Bible)

● a short **reflection** on the theme from a contemporary Christian writer

● some **questions** to address together

● a **"journeying on"** section

● some **closing prayers**

● finally, there are selected quotations from the great tradition of Christian writing to aid further reflection.

You will find a greater emphasis in the Grow stage on learning to tell the story of God's work in your life to others as every disciple is called to be a witness. You will also find a greater emphasis on learning to live out your faith in everyday life. The Journeying On section includes an individual challenge for the week ahead, and you are encouraged to share your progress as part of the Conversation as you meet for the next session.

INTRODUCTION TO *THE CREEDS*

> If you confess with your lips that Jesus is Lord and believe in your heart that God raised him from the dead, you will be saved.
>
> **ROMANS 10:9**

From the earliest days of the Church, Christians developed short, simple summaries of the faith. Many of them are embedded in the Scriptures.

These short statements became known as creeds. The word "creed" comes from the Latin word *credo*, meaning "I believe and trust." Two creeds in particular were developed in the early centuries of the Church that have remained important to the Church and are regularly used in our worship today. Both are printed at the end of this Introduction.

The **Apostles' Creed** is a faithful summary of the apostles' teaching. It begins with the clear statement: "I believe..." It declares the faith of the Church in an easily accessible way in a simple threefold structure. Many of its individual words and phrases echo the Scriptures. This is the faith of the Church which every believer declares at his or her baptism and by which we live. According to tradition, it was the creed used in the Church in Rome from earliest times.

The **Nicene Creed** is a more detailed summary of what the whole Church believes about the great doctrines of the Christian faith. It begins with the statement: "We believe..." The Nicene Creed uses the same threefold structure as the Apostles' Creed but goes into more depth and detail. It was first adopted at the Council of Nicaea in 325 CE by a gathering of bishops called the first ecumenical council.

In the early centuries of the Church, a number of different teachings arose around key questions of Christian belief. How is God one and yet three persons: Father, Son, and Holy Spirit? Is Jesus fully God and fully human? Is the Holy Spirit one with the Father and the Son?

As we read the pages of the New Testament, it is possible to see the beginnings of the debate around what is the right and true understanding of these questions. In the fifteenth chapter of the Acts of the Apostles, the early Church leaders, meeting together in Jerusalem, have to settle the question of whether keeping the Jewish law is essential to salvation. In Acts 19 Paul comes across some disciples who have not even heard that there is a Holy Spirit. In Colossians 1 Paul builds a strong case that Christ shares fully in the divine nature because there were people arguing that he did not.

The Church continued to wrestle with these issues, sometimes in fierce controversy. The early Christians sought the guidance of the Holy Spirit, and they took counsel together. They studied and pondered the Scriptures. They used their understanding and reason as gifts given by God. Finally they reached agreement at Nicaea (a city in what is today Turkey) on the fundamental shape of the Christian gospel and the defining doctrines of the Christian faith.

In the centuries following the first ecumenical council, the Church has become divided. The divisions are mainly about secondary matters. All the major traditions continue to use the words of the Apostles' Creed and the Nicene Creed in their worship and teaching.

Every time we come to say the creeds it is vital to reflect and remember *how* it is that we come to believe them. It is by the grace and mercy of God that we have come to faith and are able to say and explore these words. It is not through human cleverness or ingenuity. The Christian faith is not a human invention. There are signs of God's existence and handiwork in creation for anyone to read (Acts 14:15-17). But we believe in the way we believe because God has come to seek us out and has become known to us. God is revealed through the Scriptures and most clearly through the gift of God's Son, Jesus Christ, through the work of the Holy Spirit:

> Long ago God spoke to our ancestors in many and various ways by the prophets, but in these last days he has spoken to us by a Son, whom he appointed heir of all things, through whom he also created

the worlds. He is the reflection of God's glory and the exact imprint of God's very being, and he sustains all things by his powerful word.

HEBREWS 1:1–3

When we say the creeds we are not summarizing a human creation but the story of God's great good news for all that God has made. We also need to remember that we are declaring not our own set of personal, individual beliefs but the faith of the Church: we believe as part of the great company of faithful Christians down the ages. As we speak these words we do so as part of the worldwide family of Christian believers, the household of God. This precious faith has been passed on to us by the Church, our fellow Christians. In the same way we have the responsibility to pass it on faithfully to others.

Exploring the creeds today can seem a little daunting, especially for someone who is still fairly new to Christian faith. Think of the creeds as a great picnic basket full of good things. Each one needs to be unpacked and unwrapped, tasted, and savored. This takes time but more than repays the work involved. Or think of the creeds as the desktop of a computer or tablet, full of icons. Behind each one is a whole world of meaning to be explored—and they all connect together.

Each of the sessions in this course is one item in the basket, one icon on the desktop. In Session 1, we look at what it means to say: "I believe" and "We believe" and at the role the creeds play in strengthening our relationship with God. We move on in Session 2 to explore what it means to understand God as Trinity: one God in three persons. Sessions 3 and 4 take us deeper in our understanding of Jesus and look at the way Christ is fully God and fully human and at the great work of redemption on the cross. Session 5 explores the person and work of the Holy Spirit, and Session 6 looks at what we believe about the Church—the people of God called into being through God's grace.

Unpacking the picnic basket through this short course will equip you with priceless resources for living the Christian life, understanding the faith, and knowing God better. May God bless you as you begin this next part of the journey.

The Apostles' Creed

I believe in God, the Father almighty,
   creator of heaven and earth.

I believe in Jesus Christ, his only Son, our Lord,
   who was conceived by the Holy Spirit,
   born of the Virgin Mary,
   suffered under Pontius Pilate,
   was crucified, died, and was buried;
   he descended to the dead.
   On the third day he rose again;
   he ascended into heaven,
   he is seated at the right hand of the Father,
   and he will come to judge the living and the dead.

I believe in the Holy Spirit,
   the holy catholic Church,
   the communion of saints,
   the forgiveness of sins,
   the resurrection of the body,
   and the life everlasting. Amen.

The Nicene Creed

We believe in one God,
   the Father, the Almighty,
   maker of heaven and earth,
   of all that is, seen and unseen.

We believe in one Lord, Jesus Christ,
   the only Son of God,
   eternally begotten of the Father,
   God from God, Light from Light,
   true God from true God,
   begotten, not made,
   of one Being with the Father;
   through him all things were made.
   For us and for our salvation he came down from heaven,
   was incarnate from the Holy Spirit and the Virgin Mary
   and was made man.
For our sake he was crucified under Pontius Pilate;
   he suffered death and was buried.
   On the third day he rose again
   in accordance with the Scriptures;
   he ascended into heaven
   and is seated at the right hand of the Father.
He will come again in glory to judge the living and the dead,
   and his kingdom will have no end.

We believe in the Holy Spirit,
   the Lord, the giver of life,
   who proceeds from the Father and the Son,
   who with the Father and the Son is worshiped and glorified,
   who has spoken through the prophets.
   We believe in one holy catholic and apostolic Church.
   We acknowledge one baptism for the forgiveness of sins.
   We look for the resurrection of the dead,
     and the life of the world to come. Amen.

The Lord's Prayer

Our Father in heaven,
hallowed be your name,
your kingdom come,
your will be done,
on earth as in heaven.
Give us today our daily bread.
Forgive us our sins
as we forgive those who sin against us.
Save us from the time of trial
and deliver us from evil.
For the kingdom, the power,
and the glory are yours
now and for ever. Amen.

CONTEMPORARY LANGUAGE VERSION

Our Father, who art in heaven,
hallowed be thy name;
thy kingdom come;
thy will be done;
on earth as it is in heaven.
Give us this day our daily bread.
And forgive us our trespasses,
as we forgive those who trespass against us.
And lead us not into temptation;
but deliver us from evil.
For thine is the kingdom,
the power, and the glory,
for ever and ever. Amen.

TRADITIONAL LANGUAGE VERSION

(For use in the Concluding Prayers of each session)

SESSION ONE:
WHAT ARE THE CREEDS?

pilgrim

In this session we explore the reason the Creeds were developed and the role they play in Christian life and faith.

Opening Prayers

The heavens declare the glory of God,
And the firmament shows his handiwork.
One day tells its tale to another,
and one night imparts knowledge to another.

Although they have no words or language,
and their voices are not heard,
Their sound has gone out into all lands,
and their message to the ends of the world.

In the deep has he set a pavilion for the sun;
it comes forth like a bridegroom out of his chamber;
it rejoices like a champion to run its course.

It goes forth from the uttermost edge of the heavens
and runs about to the end of it again;
nothing is hidden from its burning heat.

PSALM 19:1-6

Eternal God, the light of the minds that know you, the joy of the
hearts that love you, and the strength of the wills that serve you:
grant us so to know you that we may truly love you, so to love you
that we may truly serve you, whose service is perfect freedom;
through Jesus Christ our Lord. **Amen.**

AFTER AUGUSTINE OF HIPPO (354–430)

Conversation

Who are your great heroes or models of faith? They may be characters
from the Bible or people from history or people you know.

Reflecting on Scripture

Reading

Now faith is the assurance of things hoped for, the conviction of things not seen. [2]Indeed, by faith our ancestors received approval. [3]By faith we understand that the worlds were prepared by the word of God, so that what is seen was made from things that are not visible.

[4]By faith Abel offered to God a more acceptable sacrifice than Cain's. Through this he received approval as righteous, God himself giving approval to his gifts; he died, but through his faith he still speaks. [5]By faith Enoch was taken so that he did not experience death; and "he was not found, because God had taken him." For it was attested before he was taken away that "he had pleased God." [6]And without faith it is impossible to please God, for whoever would approach him must believe that he exists and that he rewards those who seek him. [7]By faith Noah, warned by God about events as yet unseen, respected the warning and built an ark to save his household; by this he condemned the world and became an heir to the righteousness that is in accordance with faith.

[8]By faith Abraham obeyed when he was called to set out for a place that he was to receive as an inheritance; and he set out, not knowing where he was going. [9]By faith he stayed for a time in the land he had been promised, as in a foreign land, living in tents, as did Isaac and Jacob, who were heirs with him of the same promise. [10]For he looked forward to the city that has foundations, whose architect and builder is God.

HEBREWS 11:1-10

Explanatory note

The word translated here as "faith" could also be translated as "belief." Why not reread the passage inserting "belief" instead of "faith" and see if it feels any different? Hebrews 11 tells the story of some key Old Testament characters from Genesis who all displayed faith:

Cain and Abel were the sons of Adam and Eve (Genesis 4:1-16).

Enoch is mentioned only briefly in Genesis 5:24 and is said to have been "no more" because God took him. Out of this brief reference grew speculation about what happened to him after God took him. This speculation can be found written down outside the Bible in books such as 1 Enoch.

The story of Noah and the flood can be found in Genesis 6–9.

The story of the call of Abraham begins in Genesis 12 and continues for many chapters after that.

- Read the passage through once.
- Keep a few moments' silence.
- Read the passage a second time with different voices.
- Invite everyone to say aloud a word or phrase that strikes them.
- Read the passage a third time.
- Share together what this word or phrase might mean and what questions it raises.

Reflection
STEVEN CROFT

Belief and trust

Christians recite the creeds as part of our worship regularly, but we don't always understand what we are doing. There is more going on here than agreeing together on the content of our faith or reminding one another about orthodox Christian doctrine.

The key lies in very first words of the creed: "I believe" in the Apostles' Creed and "We believe" in the Nicene Creed. The word "believe" means far more than to agree with something or to give assent to it. It carries much more of the meaning of placing my trust and confidence in something. Remember the replies the candidates make to the questions in baptism:

Do you believe in God the Father?
I believe in God, the Father almighty, creator of heaven and earth.

Do you believe in Jesus Christ, his only Son, our Lord?
I believe in Jesus Christ, his only Son, our Lord.
He was conceived by the power of the Holy Spirit and born of the Virgin Mary.
He suffered under Pontius Pilate, was crucified, died, and was buried.
He descended to the dead.
On the third day he rose again.
He ascended into heaven, and is seated at the right hand of the Father.
He will come again to judge the living and the dead.

Do you believe in the Holy Spirit?
I believe in the Holy Spirit, the holy catholic Church, the communion of saints, the forgiveness of sins, the resurrection of the body, and the life everlasting.

As we stand to say the Creed week by week in public worship, we are deliberately placing our confidence once again in the living and loving God, Father, Son, and Holy Spirit. Every Sunday, every resurrection day, we make a new commitment and a new beginning.

Why is that so important? Because during the past seven days—or however long it is since we were together with God's people—our faith will not have been stable or steady. Many things will have happened in our lives. Some will have been good and deepened our sense of gratitude to God. But some will have been difficult and challenged our faith. We may have been tested by suffering or the suffering of those close to us. Our prayers may not have been answered. We may have been moved with compassion by the suffering in God's world. We may be asking deep questions of God and of our faith. We may have been hurt by those close to us or by other members of the Christian family.

For all these reasons, God's people need a clear moment, as we gather together, of belief and trust and confidence—a moment when, together, we place our faith and trust once again, at the beginning of the new week, in the living God, Father, Son, and Holy Spirit.

For discussion

- Why do you believe it is important to come to church and gather with other Christians Sunday by Sunday?

- What are the things that most commonly happen to you to disturb your faith and trust in God?

- What are the things that most help you trust in God again and move forward?

Living by faith

In Mark's Gospel, Jesus proclaims the good news of the kingdom. Jesus' call to those who would follow him had two elements: "repent, and believe the good news" (Mark 1:15). This is in some ways a once-and-for-all, life-changing event. We make a decision in private prayer and public confession of faith to be disciples of Jesus. But it is also a commitment to being changed and transformed in our minds (the core meaning of repentance), continually trusting again in God. This is exactly what happens when we gather to worship together as God's people: we repent of our sins, confess them together, and place our trust and confidence in God again as we declare our faith in the creed.

This saving faith is right at the heart of what it means to be a Christian. Paul writes over and over again in the letter to the Romans that we are not justified—set right with God—because of anything we do or any rules that we may keep. We cannot set ourselves right with God. We are justified through faith, through trusting in what God has done in and through Jesus Christ.

It is this story of God's saving love which is told and retold in the creeds. God's love has made us and all the world (creation). God's love has saved us from our sins through the death of Jesus Christ on the cross (redemption). God's love is changing us to be more like Jesus the Son and making us holy by the Holy Spirit (sanctification).

Hebrews 11 offers us a powerful description of what it means to have faith (11:1). More importantly, it gives us powerful examples of men and women who lived their lives by faith in God's promises—the way we are called to live today. Every time we say the creed we embrace that kind of faith and declare that we are determined to live by faith and not by sight.

In short

Jesus' key message was "repent, and believe in the good news." When we do, we make a commitment to a regular habit of being changed by and putting our trust in God.

For discussion

- Where are you tempted to place your confidence and trust if not in God?

- Can you describe a moment when you have wandered away from faith and trust and been restored?

Journeying On

Make a note this week of the things that happen in your daily life or in events elsewhere that disturb your faith and confidence in God. When you gather with God's people this week, offer that list to God and deliberately place your trust once again in God's promises and mercy.

Concluding Prayers

Do you believe and trust in God the Father?
I believe in God, the Father almighty, creator of heaven and earth.

Do you believe and trust in God's Son Jesus Christ?
I believe in Jesus Christ, his only Son, our Lord, who was conceived by the Holy Spirit, born of the Virgin Mary, suffered under Pontius Pilate, was crucified, died, and was buried; he descended to the dead. On the third day he rose again; he ascended into heaven, he is seated at the right hand of the Father, and he will come to judge the living and the dead.

Do you believe and trust in the Holy Spirit?
I believe in the Holy Spirit, the holy catholic Church, the communion of saints, the forgiveness of sins, the resurrection of the body, and the life everlasting. Amen.

As our Savior taught us, so we pray,
Our Father... (see p. 6)

Wisdom for the Journey

> Most people are enclosed in their mortal bodies like a snail in its shell, curled up in their obsessions after the manner of hedgehogs. They form their notion of God's blessedness taking themselves for a model.
>
> CLEMENT OF ALEXANDRIA (*C.* 140–*C.* 220)

> Every concept formed by the intellect in an attempt to comprehend and circumscribe the divine nature can succeed only in fashioning an idol, not in making God known.
>
> GREGORY OF NYSSA (*C.* 330–94)

> Thirst was made for water; inquiry for truth.
>
> C. S. LEWIS (1898–1963)

GOD AS TRINITY—FATHER, SON, AND HOLY SPIRIT

pilgrim

In this session we explore the profound and wonderful truth that God is Trinity: three persons in relationship, Father, Son, and Holy Spirit.

Opening Prayers

For God alone my soul in silence awaits;
from him comes my salvation.
He alone is my rock and my salvation,
my stronghold, so that I shall not be greatly shaken.

For God alone my soul in silence waits;
truly, my hope is in him.
He alone is my rock and my salvation,
my stronghold, so that I shall not be shaken.

In God is my safety and my honor;
God is my strong rock and my refuge.
Put your trust in him always, O people,
pour out your hearts before him, for God is our refuge.

PSALM 62:1-2, 5-8

Eternal light, shine into our hearts, eternal goodness, deliver us
from evil, eternal power, be our support, eternal wisdom, scatter
the darkness of our ignorance, eternal pity, have mercy upon
us; that with all our heart and mind and soul and strength we may
seek your face and be brought by your infinite mercy to your holy
presence, through Jesus Christ our Lord.

ALCUIN OF YORK (735–804)

Conversation

As you look back over the last week, can you see any patterns of
God's work in your life and any movements of repentance and faith,
disorientation and reorientation?

What were your earliest pictures of God when you first came to
faith? How have they developed and deepened over your life?

Reflecting on Scripture

Reading

Paul, an apostle of Christ Jesus by the will of God,
To the saints who are in Ephesus and are faithful in Christ Jesus:
²Grace to you and peace from God our Father and the Lord Jesus
Christ.
³Blessed be the God and Father of our Lord Jesus Christ, who has
blessed us in Christ with every spiritual blessing in the heavenly
places, ⁴just as he chose us in Christ before the foundation of the
world to be holy and blameless before him in love. ⁵He destined
us for adoption as his children through Jesus Christ, according
to the good pleasure of his will, ⁶to the praise of his glorious grace
that he freely bestowed on us in the Beloved. ⁷In him we have
redemption through his blood, the forgiveness of our trespasses,
according to the riches of his grace ⁸that he lavished on us. With
all wisdom and insight ⁹he has made known to us the mystery
of his will, according to his good pleasure that he set forth in
Christ, ¹⁰as a plan for the fullness of time, to gather up all things
in him, things in heaven and things on earth. ¹¹In Christ we have
also obtained an inheritance, having been destined according
to the purpose of him who accomplishes all things according to
his counsel and will, ¹²so that we, who were the first to set our
hope on Christ, might live for the praise of his glory. ¹³In him you
also, when you had heard the word of truth, the gospel of your
salvation, and had believed in him, were marked with the seal of
the promised Holy Spirit; ¹⁴this is the pledge of our inheritance
towards redemption as God's own people, to the praise of his glory.

EPHESIANS 1:1-14

Explanatory note

One of the remarkable features of this passage that cannot be communicated by
English translations is that verses 3-14 are a single sentence focused around God,
Jesus Christ, and the Holy Spirit.
Try reading the whole lot with one breath and see how it feels.

Notice how often "he," "in him," and "in Christ" are used. What words could we substitute for "him" to expand our understanding of God beyond the masculine? "Blessed be the God..." is the phrase often used at the start of Jewish prayers even today.

- Read the passage through once.
- Keep a few moments' silence.
- Read the passage a second time with different voices.
- Invite everyone to say aloud a word or phrase that strikes them.
- Read the passage a third time.
- Share together what this word or phrase might mean and what questions it raises.

Reflection   JANE WILLIAMS

God, Father, Son, and Holy Spirit

The life, death, and resurrection of Jesus Christ draws us into a belief that God is Father, Son, and Holy Spirit. The earliest Christians tried to make sense of what had happened in Jesus. They became convinced that, in Jesus, we encounter not just a message *about* God but the activity and presence *of God in person*. They discovered that God's activity and presence is not withdrawn again when the earthly Jesus ascends to the Father. Instead, the presence of God remains where believers gather in the name of Jesus to worship and honor the Father: we are held in the presence and activity of God by God's own "seal," as Ephesians puts it: the Holy Spirit.

> *The presence of God remains where believers gather.*

With the early Christians, we look today at Jesus, at God taking flesh and dwelling among us. At the heart of what we see is this relationship of love, trust, and united purpose between Father, Son, and Holy Spirit.

The Father entrusts the work of the kingdom to the Son. The Holy Spirit builds the fruits of the kingdom in the Son's community, the Church. The result of Jesus' preaching of the kingdom is a new community. God's own reality is all about relationships. The very terms "Father," "Son," and "Holy Spirit" are not proper names or descriptions of functions but terms that describe relationships. The persons of the Trinity are not interchangeable, nor do they "do" different things: simply, the Father is the Father of the Son, and the Holy Spirit is the love that makes God three and one.

It is only because we know that God is Trinity that we can say that God *is* love. It would otherwise be possible to surmise that God is loving, or acts lovingly, but to say that God *is* love is only possible for this reason: because within the very being of God is the relationship between three persons and the self-giving that characterizes love.

> *We can say that God is love.*

In short

The relationship of love and self-giving within the Trinity itself—Father (as a parent), Son, and Holy Spirit—allows us to say that God is love.

For discussion

- If a relationship of love between Father, Son, and Holy Spirit is at the very heart of God's nature, what does that teach us about the way we should relate to one another in the life of the Church?

- Which person of the Trinity do you find it hardest to engage with? Why do you think that might be?

- What other term beside "Father" could you use to describe God?

Understanding God's nature

Christians came to an understanding and belief in God as Trinity only after experiencing God in Jesus Christ. However, what is striking is that this understanding confirms—and indeed makes possible—convictions about God that had long been believed. The encounter with

God as Trinity is both shockingly new and yet somehow characteristic of the God already revealed in the Hebrew Scriptures.

Genesis says that God is creator and that God creates freely and with joy. So it is not so strange that God the Son should come to live in and affirm the work of the creator, or that God the Spirit should continue to draw created beings into that relationship for which they were made. The Trinitarian God is able and willing to be faithful to creatures and to God's own creative nature. God can do this because God is not a simple, undifferentiated being but a unity-in-relation. It is not alien to God to be in relation: God in relation is the heart of all reality.

Christians contrast the idea that God is above and beyond all things (God's transcendence) with the idea that God indwells every part of the creation (God's immanence). It is because God is three and one that God can be both transcendent and utterly unknowable—and also intimately present.

If God were not Trinity, how could we know about God? We could learn about God through the creation, but that means that knowledge of God would only come to us through what is not God. Alternatively, our knowledge of God could, somehow, be imposed directly by God, bypassing human cooperation. But the Trinitarian God is able to hold together transcendence and immanence because this God is already outpouring and returning relationship in God's very being.

To come to "know" God, then, is to be drawn into this relationship that God enables. God makes room for us, as the body of the Son, the body of Christ, filled with the breath of God, the Holy Spirit. There is no abstract knowledge of God, only participatory life in God.

Just as, in God, Father, Son, and Holy Spirit are one yet distinct, so it is in the body of Christ. We rejoice at our unity-in-diversity, glorying in our interdependence, reveling in the variety of gifts with which this body is endowed.

Ephesians says that this new community, the body of the Son, held in being by the Spirit, is a body with a purpose. We live "for the praise of his glory" (Ephesians 1:12,

We are the advance party.

14). We are the advance party, living in the hope of what is to come, when the faithfulness of God, the creator, redeemer, and fulfiller, will "gather up all things in him, things in heaven and things on earth" (Ephesians 1:10). When all things are gathered into God, they will not cease to be but instead will find their true reality, which is to share in the abundance of the life of God, Father, Son, and Holy Spirit.

In short

We are able to participate in the abundant life of God through the relationship that exists between Father, Son, and Holy Spirit.

For discussion

- Do you find it easier to think about God above everything or God in everything?

- Which "person" of the Trinity do you find yourself thinking about most and which least? How does this vary within the group?

Journeying On

Look back over the passage in Ephesians 1 and the Reflection each day this week.

Each day try to find something new to thank God for about the nature of God as Trinity: Father, Son, and Holy Spirit.

Concluding Prayers

Let us declare our faith in God.

We believe in God the Father,
from whom every family in heaven and on earth is named.
We believe in God the Son,
who lives in our hearts through faith, and fills us with his love.
We believe in God the Holy Spirit,
who strengthens us with power from on high.
We believe in one God;
Father, Son, and Holy Spirit.
Amen.   BASED ON EPHESIANS 3

As our Savior taught us, so we pray,
Our Father... (see p. 6)

Wisdom for the Journey

Our detractors proclaim our madness because we honor a
crucified man alongside the unchangeable and eternal God, the
creator of all. They do not discern the mystery in this, and it is to
this mystery that we beg you attend.

JUSTIN (*C.* 100–165)

The glory of God is a human being fully alive, and the life of
humanity consists in the vision of God.

IRENAEUS (*C.* 130–*C.* 200)

The one thing that matters is that we always say "Yes" to God
whenever we experience him, and really do well to be with him
with all our heart and soul and strength.

JULIAN OF NORWICH (1373–1417)

There's a divinity that shapes our ends,
Rough-hew them how we will.

WILLIAM SHAKESPEARE (1564–1616)

FULLY GOD AND FULLY HUMAN

pilgrim ————————————————————————

In this session we explore the unique nature of Jesus Christ. Jesus is fully God and fully human. This teaches us a great deal about God and about what it is to be human.

Opening Prayers

How dear to me is your dwelling, O LORD of hosts!
my soul has a desire and longing for the courts of the LORD;
my heart and my flesh rejoice in the living God.

The sparrow has found her a house
and the swallow a nest where she may lay her young;
by the side of your altars, O LORD of hosts, my King and my God.

Happy are they who dwell in your house!
they will always be praising you.

Happy are the people whose strength is in you!
whose hearts are set on the pilgrims' way.

PSALM 84:1-4

Christ be with me, Christ within me, Christ behind me, Christ before
me, Christ beside me, Christ to win me, Christ to comfort and
restore me, Christ beneath me, Christ above me, Christ in quiet,
Christ in danger, Christ in hearts of all that love me, Christ in mouth
of friend and stranger.

FROM ST PATRICK'S BREASTPLATE

Conversation

Last week the group was asked to reflect on the different things you
want to give thanks for about God's nature as Trinity. What can you
share with the group about this?

Looking ahead to this week, which is your favorite Gospel and why?

Reflecting on Scripture

Reading

In the beginning was the Word, and the Word was with God, and the Word was God. [2]He was in the beginning with God. [3]All things came into being through him, and without him not one thing came into being. What has come into being [4]in him was life, and the life was the light of all people. [5]The light shines in the darkness, and the darkness did not overcome it.

[6]There was a man sent from God, whose name was John. [7]He came as a witness to testify to the light, so that all might believe through him. [8]He himself was not the light, but he came to testify to the light. [9]The true light, which enlightens everyone, was coming into the world.

[10]He was in the world, and the world came into being through him; yet the world did not know him. [11]He came to what was his own, and his own people did not accept him. [12]But to all who received him, who believed in his name, he gave power to become children of God, [13]who were born, not of blood or of the will of the flesh or of the will of man, but of God.

[14]And the Word became flesh and lived among us, and we have seen his glory, the glory as of a father's only son, full of grace and truth.

JOHN 1:1-14

Explanatory note

Many people view this passage as an early poem, hymn, or creedal statement that might have been used in the early Church to express what they believed about Jesus Christ the Word.

This passage has many links with the creation story in Genesis 1, not least its opening "In the beginning."

John's Gospel is the only Gospel to link Jesus with "the Word." It is an idea rich with meaning. Just as words leave our mouths and give effect to our thoughts, so Jesus reveals who God really is.

- Read the passage through once.
- Keep a few moments' silence.
- Read the passage a second time with different voices.
- Invite everyone to say aloud a word or phrase that strikes them.
- Read the passage a third time.
- Share together what this word or phrase might mean and what questions it raises.

Reflection

STEPHEN COTTRELL

And the Word became flesh

Some Christians talk about Jesus as if he were a superhero, a kind of spiritual superman able to call upon supernatural powers at any time to do anything he wanted. But there are all sorts of occasions in the Gospels that question such a view. When Jesus goes to his home town, he is not able to work any miracle there. In the Garden of Gethsemane he prays that there might be another way. On the cross he submits to suffering and death and does not satisfy the crowds who mock him saying, "Save yourself! If you are the Son of God, come down from the cross."

Others—often those outside the Church but some Christians as well—talk about Jesus as if he is just a man. They speak of him as a great teacher, a great philosopher, an inspiring leader, an exemplary human being. But such an account of Jesus ignores the signs and wonders that he does perform, not least the greatest miracle of all, his resurrection from the dead.

So who is Jesus, and how should we talk about him?

John's Gospel, as we have just seen, begins with the dramatic assertion that, in Jesus, God's word, the word of God that was with God from the beginning, has become flesh.

The word the Church uses to describe this is "incarnation." It means "enfleshed." In Jesus, God has come down to earth and dwells among us in the likeness and substance of our own humanity. As the letter to the Philippians puts it, Jesus, "though he was in the form of God, did not regard equality with God as something to be exploited, but emptied himself, taking the form of a slave, being born in human likeness. And being found in human form, he humbled himself and became obedient to the point of death—even death on a cross" (Philippians 2:6-8).

In other words, Jesus shares completely what it is to be human. God comes to us and speaks to us in the language of another human life. Thus Jesus is completely human and completely God. He is the meeting point between our frail and mortal flesh and the everlasting life of God. In him, life and death, heaven and earth, humanity and God unite. Jesus is not just a perfect human being, he is fully God. Jesus is not God in the disguise of a human being, he is fully human. In his one person are two natures—God and man (human).

> *In him, life and death, heaven and earth, humanity and God unite.*

Athanasius, one of the great teachers of the Church and someone who defended this orthodox Christian view against those who would make Jesus more God than man, wrote: "He became what we are so that we could become what he is." For unless Jesus is one of us, he can be our judge but not our savior. On the cross, Jesus who is God defeats sin and death. On the cross, Jesus who is man shares the consequences of that sin and dies a sinner's death. He who is without sin becomes sin for us. He who is the source of life experiences death.

In short
We believe that Jesus was God but also fully human. It was only by becoming fully human that he could save us.

For discussion

- Make a list together—on paper or in conversation—about the stories in the Gospels that most show Jesus is fully human. Then make a list of those that most show Jesus is fully God.

- If Jesus were only a very good man or God dressed up as a human being, what difference do you think this would make?

Conceived by the Holy Spirit, born of the Virgin Mary

The incarnation is therefore one of the foundational beliefs of the Christian faith. In the creed we affirm our belief in Jesus "the only Son of God" but also the one who "for us and for our salvation came down from heaven" and "was incarnate from the Holy Spirit and the Virgin Mary" and made man.

Mary is specifically mentioned because she acts as one of the safeguards of this belief. We honor Mary because of her vital place in the story of salvation. In defense of Christ's true humanity, the Church emphasizes Jesus' birth from Mary. He is a "man of the substance of his Mother," affirms the Athanasian Creed. The one born of Mary is the eternal Son of God. Jesus was "conceived by the Holy Spirit" and "born of the Virgin Mary," declares the Apostles' Creed. For these reasons Mary is sometimes called *theotokos*, a Greek title meaning "God-bearer."

Finally, and very practically, belief in the incarnation changes the way we think about each other and the world around us. It means that the created matter of the universe, our own human flesh, and every person we ever meet have been blessed by God. They are holy. They are the places where God has chosen to dwell. The Christian faith is very down to earth.

In short

The incarnation is one of the central beliefs of Christianity. It is important not just because it tells us something about Jesus but because it tells us something about all human beings—because Jesus became human, all humanity has been blessed by God.

For discussion

- How do you think of Mary and of her role in salvation?
- How does belief in the incarnation change the way we think about each other and the world around us?
- What does it mean to love the world in the same way Jesus loves the world?

Journeying On

"The Word became flesh and lived among us" (John 1:14). One of the ways we live out our faith is "being with" people in the name of Christ.

Who will you "be with" this week in your family, your daily work, or your other activities? Think about what it means to be with them in the name of Christ and as a bearer of Christ's name. Make a list during the week of people you notice "being with" in this way.

Concluding Prayers

Let us affirm our faith in Jesus Christ the Son of God.

Though he was divine, he did not cling to equality with God, but made himself nothing. Taking the form of a slave, he was born in human likeness. He humbled himself and was obedient to death, even the death of the cross. Therefore God has raised him on high, and given him the name above every name: that at the name of Jesus, every knee should bow, and every voice proclaim that Jesus Christ is Lord, to the glory of God the Father. Amen.

BASED ON PHILIPPIANS 2:6-11

As our Savior taught us, so we pray,
Our Father... (see p. 6)

Wisdom for the Journey

God so loved us that for our sakes he, through whom time was made, was made in time; older by eternity than the world itself, he became younger in age than many of his servants in the world; God, who made man, was made man; he was given existence by a mother whom he brought into existence; he was carried in hands which he formed; he was nursed at breasts which he filled; he cried like a baby in the manger in speechless infancy—this Word without which human eloquence is speechless.

AUGUSTINE (354–430)

When God emptied himself and took the form of a servant, he emptied himself of majesty and power, not of goodness and mercy. God's power had appeared already in creation, and his wisdom in the ordering of creation; but his goodness and mercy have appeared now in his humanity. So what are you frightened of? God has come not to judge the world, but to save it! Do not run away; do not be afraid. God comes unarmed; he wants to save you, not to punish you. And lest you should say "I heard your voice and I hid myself," look: he is here, an infant with no voice. The cry of a baby is something to be pitied, not to be frightened of. He is made a little child, the Virgin Mother has wrapped his tender limbs in swaddling bands; so why are you still quaking with fear? This tells you that God has come to save you, not to lose you; to rescue you, not to imprison you.

BERNARD OF CLAIRVAUX (1090–1153)

In Christ I meet the real God. In him I find no metaphysical abstraction, but God speaking to me in the only language I can understand which is the human language.

GEOFFREY STUDDERT KENNEDY (1883–1929)

We often feel we ought to get on quickly to a new stage like spiritual mayflies. Christ takes thirty years to grow and two and a half to act.

EVELYN UNDERHILL (1875–1941)

SESSION FOUR:
CRUCIFIED, RISEN, AND ASCENDED

pilgrim ——————————————

In this session we explore the great shadows in our lives—sin and death and hell—and the way Jesus overcomes these through his death and resurrection.

Opening Prayers

I lift up my eyes to the hills;
from where is my help to come?

**My help comes from the LORD,
the maker of heaven and earth.**

He will not let your foot be moved
and he who watches over you will not fall asleep.

**Behold, he who keeps watch over Israel
shall neither slumber nor sleep.**

PSALM 121:1-4

Lord Jesus Christ, we thank you for all the benefits you have won for
us, for all the pains and insults you have borne for us. Most merciful
redeemer, friend and brother, may we know you more clearly, love
you more dearly, and follow you more nearly, day by day.

AFTER RICHARD OF CHICHESTER (1253)

Conversation

**Look back over the last week. Who were the people you spent time
with? What difference did it make to be with them in the name of
Christ and in the pattern of the incarnation? Did you act or speak
differently?**

**Do you have a favorite representation of the cross in jewelry, in a
work of art, or in a church building?**

Reflecting on Scripture

Israel (handwritten)

Reading

Who has believed what we have heard? And to whom has the arm of the LORD been revealed? [2]For he grew up before him like a young plant, and like a root out of dry ground; he had no form or majesty that we should look at him, nothing in his appearance that we should desire him. [3]He was despised and rejected by others; a man of suffering and acquainted with infirmity; and as one from whom others hide their faces he was despised, and we held him of no account.

[4]Surely he has borne our infirmities and carried our diseases; yet we accounted him stricken, struck down by God, and afflicted. [5]But he was wounded for our transgressions, crushed for our iniquities; upon him was the punishment that made us whole, and by his bruises we are healed. [6]All we like sheep have gone astray; we have all turned to our own way, and the LORD has laid on him the iniquity of us all.

[7]He was oppressed, and he was afflicted, yet he did not open his mouth; like a lamb that is led to the slaughter, and like a sheep that before its shearers is silent, so he did not open his mouth. [8]By a perversion of justice he was taken away. Who could have imagined his future? For he was cut off from the land of the living, stricken for the transgression of my people. [9]They made his grave with the wicked and his tomb with the rich, although he had done no violence, and there was no deceit in his mouth. [10]Yet it was the will of the LORD to crush him with pain. When you make his life an offering for sin, he shall see his offspring, and shall prolong his days; through him the will of the LORD shall prosper. [11]Out of his anguish he shall see light; he shall find satisfaction through his knowledge. The righteous one, my servant, shall make many righteous, and he shall bear their iniquities. [12]Therefore I will allot him a portion with the great, and he shall divide the spoil with the strong; because he poured out himself to death, and was numbered with the transgressors;

yet he bore the sin of many, and made intercession for the
transgressors.

ISAIAH 53:1-12

Explanatory note

This passage is often called a "Servant Song" and is associated with four others in
Isaiah (42:1-4; 49:1-6; 50:4-9; and 52:13–53:12). All four Servant Songs focus on the
role of a "Servant" in carrying out God's mission in the world.

This song very quickly became associated with Jesus in the early Church and was
used in Acts 8:27-38 by Philip to explain the good news of Jesus.

- Read the passage through once—though as this is a longer
  passage than usual you may decide to omit the first reading.

- Keep a few moments' silence.

- Read the passage a second time with different voices.

- Invite everyone to say aloud a word or phrase that strikes them.

- Read the passage a third time.

- Share together what this word or phrase might mean and what
  questions it raises.

Reflection   GRAHAM TOMLIN

Crucified, dead, and buried

When we think deeply about life in our more honest moments, a
number of shadows lurk in the background. We hurt each other badly.
We damage the world we live in. Our lives are characterized far too
often by pride, envy, anger, greed, lust, and other destructive habits.

This is the shadow that the Bible calls *sin*, a crime not just against the
people that we hurt with our selfishness but against the God whose
image we all bear. Second, there is the shadow of *death*—the one thing
that can be said for sure about the future is that one day we are all
destined to die. A third shadow is the question of *direction*. Many people

struggle with a lack of purpose, not knowing where they are going in this life or the next. Does it all end in life or in death? heaven or hell?

One of the strange things about the Gospels is the disproportionate amount of space they give to the last week of Jesus' life. In John's Gospel, for example, 10 out of the 21 chapters are given over to describing his final few days.

The Apostles' Creed tells us that Jesus:
...suffered under Pontius Pilate,
was crucified, died and was buried.
He descended to the dead.
On the third day he rose again.
He ascended into heaven
and is seated at the right hand of the Father.

The purpose of these events at the end of Jesus' life is the banishing of these three shadows of sin, of death, and of futility, and the dawning of light.

First, Jesus dies. Just 20 or so years later, when Paul wrote to the young church in Corinth, he interpreted the death of Jesus as something much more significant than yet another Jewish rebel crucified by the Romans: "Christ died *for our sins* in accordance with the scriptures" (1 Corinthians 15:3). It was perhaps texts such as the one in Isaiah 53 that Paul had in mind—texts that foretold a figure who would, in some sense, be "stricken for the transgression of my people."

When a deep offense has been committed, justice has to be done. We as a human race have to atone for our sin of turning away from God, wounding each other and the creation we were supposed to look after.

Jesus dies bearing the sins of the world on his shoulders.

And this is exactly what happens: Jesus died *as one of us*. Jesus, the divine Son who has taken our human nature, dies on our behalf, as a representative of the human race, bearing the sins of the world on his shoulders.

Then something no one expected happened. First-century Jews believed that at the end of time there would be a general resurrection of the dead, but no one expected it in the middle of history. Yet three days later, Jesus was raised—the one who died as the sinless Son of God is not so much resuscitated from death only to die again one day, but passes right through death and comes out the other side.

Now, the creeds tell us, he "is seated at the right hand of the Father." His final destination is not death but intimate fellowship with his Father, reigning over all things

---

In short

Jesus' death banishes the shadows of sin and ushers in the dawning of light. Jesus died as one of us, bearing the sins of the world on his shoulders.

For discussion

- Which of these three "shadows" is most significant in modern life—sin, death, or futility? Which of them is most significant for you personally?

- "Hell" is described in the Bible as the "emptiness of nothingness." Is there a fear of that in the modern world?

- The New Testament uses various images to convey the meaning of the cross. For instance: a "ransom" or price paid to a captor to ensure the release of a captive (Mark 10:45); a law court, with acquittal pronounced over the guilty because their crime has been dealt with (for example, Romans 8:33; Colossians 2:14); the reconciliation of enemies (Romans 5:10; 2 Corinthians 5:19). Which image do you find most helpful and why?

A pattern for our lives

The trajectory of the story of Jesus' death and resurrection is important. God comes into history to exist as a person and, as a person, dies on a cross so that our sins are

> *Death need not be the end.*

fully atoned for. Jesus is then raised from death, blazing a trail for others to follow so that we can know that death need not be the end— there is a hope, the certainty of a new kind of life, that can be tasted here and now and fully enjoyed after this life is over. He then ascends to the Father, sitting on the throne of heaven so that we can know that the true destiny of humanity is not the emptiness of nothingness— what the Bible calls hell—but fellowship with God, our Creator.

This is the story of Jesus. The remarkable thing is that it can also be our story. Paul describes a Christian as someone who is "in Christ." By faith in him and through baptism into Christ, I become, as it were, part of him, so that his story becomes mine. My sins have been paid for, so I do not have to live under a constant cloud of guilt. I too have the promise of eternal life, begun here and reaching its fulfillment after death. I too am seated next to the Father in Christ, knowing God's intimate presence, love, and purpose. By being in Christ, forgiveness, new life, and a joyful future become mine. And yours.

In short

When we become Christians we become a part of Christ so that his story becomes our story.

For discussion

- In what ways do you think we can know the life of the resurrection here and now?

- How do you imagine the resurrection life? Which is your favorite image of heaven?

Journeying On

Christ's story can also be our story. At the beginning of the session we prayed: "May we know you more clearly, love you more dearly, and follow you more nearly, day by day."

Be alert as you go through the week to the ways the pattern of forgiveness and new beginnings for you and for others is woven through your life. If you can, write down some examples to share next week.

Concluding Prayers

Let us declare our faith in the resurrection of our Lord Jesus Christ.

Christ died for our sins in accordance with the Scriptures; he was buried; he was raised to life on the third day in accordance with the Scriptures; afterwards he appeared to his followers, and to all the apostles: this we have received, and this we believe. Amen.

BASED ON 1 CORINTHIANS 15:3-7

As our Savior taught us, so we pray,
Our Father... (see p. 6)

Wisdom for the Journey

The cross is a war memorial erected against the demons.

JOHN CHRYSOSTOM (C. 347–407)

What God promises us for the future is great, but what God has already done for us in Christ is greater still. Who can doubt that he will give us his life, since he has already given us his death? Why is human weakness so slow to believe that we will one day live with God? After all, a much more incredible thing has already happened: God died for us.

AUGUSTINE (354–430)

It is as if God the Father sent upon the earth a purse full of his mercy. This purse was burst open during the Lord's passion to pour forth its hidden contents: the price of our redemption. It was only a small purse, but it was very full.

BERNARD OF CLAIRVAUX (1090–1153)

Our good Lord Jesus Christ said, "If I could possibly have suffered more for you, I would have done so." In his word I saw that he would have died again and again, for his love would have given him no rest until he had done so. For though the dear humanity of Christ could only suffer once, his goodness would always make him willing to do so—every day if need be. If he were to say that for love of me he would make a new heaven and a new earth, this would be a comparatively simple matter; something he could do every day if he wanted, with no great effort. But for love of me to be willing to die times without number—beyond human capacity to compute—is, to my mind, the greatest gesture our Lord God could make to the human soul. For his suffering was a noble and most worthy deed worked out by love in time, and his love has no beginning, but is now, and ever shall be.

JULIAN OF NORWICH (1373–1417)

Rise heart; thy Lord is risen. Sing his praise
Without delays,
Who takes thee by the hand, that thou likewise
With him mayst rise:
That, as his death calcined thee to dust,
His life may make thee gold, and much more, just.

GEORGE HERBERT (1593–1633)

In moments of weakness and distress it is good to tread closely in God's footsteps.

ALEXANDER SOLZHENITSYN (1918–2008)

God does not fussily intervene to deliver us from all discomfort, but neither is he the impotent beholder of cosmic history. Patiently, subtly, with infinite respect for the creation with which he has to deal, he is at work within the flexibility of its process.

JOHN POLKINGHORNE (1930–)

I BELIEVE IN THE HOLY SPIRIT

pilgrim

In this session we explore what it means to receive the Holy Spirit and the Holy Spirit's role in the life of the Church.

Opening Prayers

Be joyful in the LORD, all you lands;
serve the LORD with gladness
and come before his presence with a song.

**Know this: The LORD himself is God;
he himself has made us, and we are his;
we are his people and the sheep of his pasture.**

Enter his gates with thanksgiving;
go into his courts with praise;
give thanks to him and call upon his Name.

**For the LORD is good; His mercy is everlasting;
and his faithfulness endures from age to age.**

PSALM 100

O gracious and holy Father, give us wisdom to perceive you,
diligence to seek you, patience to wait for you, eyes to behold you, a
heart to meditate upon you, and a life to proclaim you, through the
power of the Spirit of Jesus Christ our Lord.

BENEDICT OF NURSIA (C. 480–550)

Conversation

**Can you describe a moment over the past week or month when you
have reflected more deeply on the death and resurrection of Jesus
and what it means to you? Were there any insights into forgiveness
and new beginnings this week?**

**When did you first come to understand what it means to believe in
the Holy Spirit?**

Reflecting on Scripture

Reading

When the day of Pentecost had come, they were all together in one place. ²And suddenly from heaven there came a sound like the rush of a violent wind, and it filled the entire house where they were sitting. ³Divided tongues, as of fire, appeared among them, and a tongue rested on each of them. ⁴All of them were filled with the Holy Spirit and began to speak in other languages, as the Spirit gave them ability.

⁵Now there were devout Jews from every nation under heaven living in Jerusalem. ⁶And at this sound the crowd gathered and was bewildered, because each one heard them speaking in the native language of each. ⁷Amazed and astonished, they asked, "Are not all these who are speaking Galileans? ⁸And how is it that we hear, each of us, in our own native language?"... ¹²All were amazed and perplexed, saying to one another, "What does this mean?" ¹³But others sneered and said, "They are filled with new wine."

¹⁴But Peter, standing with the eleven, raised his voice and addressed them: "Men of Judea and all who live in Jerusalem, let this be known to you, and listen to what I say. ¹⁵Indeed, these are not drunk, as you suppose, for it is only nine o'clock in the morning. ¹⁶No, this is what was spoken through the prophet Joel: ¹⁷'In the last days it will be, God declares, that I will pour out my Spirit upon all flesh, and your sons and your daughters shall prophesy, and your young men shall see visions, and your old men shall dream dreams. ¹⁸Even upon my slaves, both men and women, in those days I will pour out my Spirit; and they shall prophesy.'"

ACTS 2:1-8, 12-18

Explanatory note

Pentecost is the Greek name for the Feast of Weeks in which the Jews celebrated the giving of the law at Sinai, one of the most important festivals. As a result there would have been Jews from all over the world in Jerusalem.

In the Old Testament God's presence is often associated with fire, wind, earthquakes, lightning, and clouds.

- Read the passage through once.
- Keep a few moments' silence.
- Read the passage a second time with different voices.
- Invite everyone to say aloud a word or phrase that strikes them.
- Read the passage a third time.
- Share together what this word or phrase might mean and what questions it raises.

Reflection   MARTYN SNOW

The Go-between God

The Apostles' Creed has little to say about the Holy Spirit. Other than the Spirit's role in the conception of Jesus Christ, the Spirit appears only in a list of beliefs alongside the Church, the saints, the forgiveness of sins, and the resurrection of the body. The Nicene Creed fills in a little more detail but leaves the impression that it is addressing certain controversies of the time rather than giving a full sense of the identity and activity of the third person of the Trinity.

While this may be unfortunate (and it is certainly true to say that there have been times in the history of the Church when the activity of the Spirit has been undervalued), it is not altogether inappropriate. One writer has referred to the Holy Spirit as "the person without a face." The Spirit is the person of the Trinity who hides their face, because the Holy Spirit's work is not to draw attention to the third person of the Trinity but to open us up to the Father and the Son. Because the Spirit is eternally one with them, and is sent by them to us, so the Spirit can bring us to them. In the words of another writer, the Holy Spirit is the "Go-between God."

Throughout the Bible the Spirit is commonly described as wind, air, or breath—all things you cannot see or know directly but only by their effects. Augustine famously used a different image, describing the Spirit as the "bond of affection" or "tie of love" between the Father and the Son. This love is then poured out on us so that we are drawn into the "circle of love." Jesus said, "Those who love me will keep my word, and my Father will love

> *We are drawn into the "circle of love."*

them, and we will come to them and make our home with them" (John 14:23).

So the Spirit makes God's love real to us and draws us into an intimate relationship with the Father and the Son. This is expressed in baptism (think of the words said over Jesus: "You are my Son, the Beloved; with you I am well pleased"), in confirmation (where the bishop prays that candidates will be filled with the Holy Spirit), in Holy Communion ("Grant that by the power of your Holy Spirit, these gifts of bread and wine may be to us his body and his blood") and in the relationships between believers in the Church ("You also are built together spiritually into a dwelling-place for God" [Ephesians 2:22]).

In short
The Holy Spirit acts as the mediator between the Father, the Son, and us, drawing us into relationship with them and into their circle of love.

For discussion

- Why do you think the writers of the creeds might have struggled to know what to say about the Holy Spirit?

- What do you find helpful about Augustine's description of the Spirit as "the bond of affection"? Are there less helpful aspects to this description?

- How should we speak of the Holy Spirit—as a person or an impersonal force? Should we use a masculine or a feminine pronoun?

Unity and diversity

Acts 2 uses striking imagery—wind and fire—to depict the coming of the Holy Spirit to the first believers. Both are familiar Old Testament images for God's presence among the people. But there is more to this story. It also dramatically reveals the unity and diversity of the new community of the Spirit. People from many nations and backgrounds are now united "in the one Spirit," and yet each hears the word of God in their own language—the Spirit enables them to receive the gifts of God within their own cultural context.

These are tremendously important themes both for the Church and wider society. Various writers have suggested that one of the most pressing questions of our time is: "Can we live together?" The forces that pull us apart and divide us are so strong. How then can we overcome the many obstacles to true community and unity?

The Bible tackles this question head on when it speaks both of the "fruit of the Spirit" (Galatians 5:22-23) and the "gifts of the Spirit" (1 Corinthians 12; Romans 12). The first is about the Spirit of Jesus forming the character of Jesus within us and within the whole Christian community. The second is about the Spirit enabling every Christian to play a unique role in building up the common life of the community. Both are essential for the formation of genuine relationships and the overcoming of deep divisions.

Such unity is not built on conformity to any one particular culture (or way of being and doing). The story of Acts is the story of the Church being prompted by the Holy Spirit to take the message of Jesus out from Jerusalem to "the ends of the earth." In doing so the Spirit challenged many cultural assumptions of the first believers and convinced them that "God shows no partiality, but in every nation anyone who fears him and does what is right is acceptable to him" (Acts 10:34-35).

> **In short**
>
> The Holy Spirit brings unity but not at the expense of diversity.
> The Spirit enables each Christian to build up the common life
> of the community but does not call for conformity to just one way
> of being.

For discussion

- Do you agree that one of the most pressing questions of our time is:"Can we live together?"

- How do the "fruit of the Spirit" and the "gifts of the Spirit" enable us to overcome divisions?

- If part of the activity of the Spirit is to prompt us to take the message of Jesus out from our own culture into other cultures, where is the Spirit leading you?

Journeying On

The first Christians experienced the gift of the Spirit as a gentle breath on the forehead and as a mighty wind; as a living spring within them and as a drenching (the root meaning of baptism).

How would you tell the story of your own experience of the Holy Spirit in your life? How thirsty are you to receive more of the Spirit's life and grace and power?

Concluding Prayers

Do you believe and trust in God the Father, source of all being and life, the one for whom we exist?
We believe and trust in him.

Do you believe and trust in God the Son, who took our human nature, died for us, and rose again?
We believe and trust in him.

Do you believe and trust in God the Holy Spirit, who gives life to the people of God and makes Christ known in the world?
We believe and trust in him.

This is the faith of the Church.
This is our faith. We believe and trust in one God, Father, Son, and Holy Spirit. Amen.

As our Savior taught us, so we pray,
Our Father... (see p. 6)

Wisdom for the Journey

When a sunbeam falls on our faces we enjoy it as though the sun shines for us alone, whereas in reality the sun is shining over land and sea and mingles in the air. In the same way, the Spirit is present to all who are open to receiving him as if given to each uniquely, and sends for grace sufficient and enough for all.

BASIL THE GREAT (*C.* 329–79)

We come to God not by navigation, but by love.

AUGUSTINE (354–430)

When the Spirit dwells within a person, from the moment that person has become prayer, the Spirit never leaves them.

ISAAC OF NINEVEH (SEVENTH CENTURY)

O blessed fire, when shall I partake of thy sacred flames? O come and take possession of my heart, consume all the bonds that tie it to the earth, and carry it up with thee towards the heavenly furnace from whence thou comest.

RICHARD CHALLONER (1691–1781)

SESSION SIX:
ONE, HOLY, CATHOLIC, AND APOSTOLIC CHURCH

pilgrim

In this session we explore what it means to belong to the people of God and to declare that the Church is one, holy, catholic, and apostolic.

Session
SIX

49

Opening Prayers

Bless the Lord, O my soul,
and all this is within me, bless his holy Name.

**Bless the Lord, O my soul,
and forget not all his benefits.**

He forgives all your sins
and heals all your infirmities;

**He redeems your life from the grave
and crowns you with mercy and loving-kindness;**

He satisfies you with good things,
and your youth is renewed like an eagle's.

PSALM 103:1-5

O Lord, you have given us your word for a light to shine upon our
path. Grant us so to meditate on that word, and to follow its teaching,
that we may find in it the light that shines more and more until the
perfect day; through Jesus Christ our Lord. **Amen.**

AFTER JEROME (357–420)

Conversation

**Tell part of the story of your experience of the Holy Spirit's work
across your life and especially in recent years.**

What is your earliest positive memory of the Church?

Reflecting on Scripture

Rid yourselves, therefore, of all malice, and all guile, insincerity, envy, and all slander. [2]Like newborn infants, long for the pure, spiritual milk, so that by it you may grow into salvation—[3]if indeed you have tasted that the Lord is good.
[4]Come to him, a living stone, though rejected by mortals yet chosen and precious in God's sight, and [5]like living stones, let yourselves be built into a spiritual house, to be a holy priesthood, to offer spiritual sacrifices acceptable to God through Jesus Christ. [6]For it stands in scripture: "See, I am laying in Zion a stone, a cornerstone chosen and precious; and whoever believes in him will not be put to shame." [7]To you then who believe, he is precious; but for those who do not believe, "The stone that the builders rejected has become the very head of the corner," [8]and "A stone that makes them stumble, and a rock that makes them fall." They stumble because they disobey the word, as they were destined to do.
[9]But you are a chosen race, a royal priesthood, a holy nation, God's own people, in order that you may proclaim the mighty acts of him who called you out of darkness into his marvelous light. [10]Once you were not a people, but now you are God's people; once you had not received mercy, but now you have received mercy.
[11]Beloved, I urge you as aliens and exiles to abstain from the desires of the flesh that wage war against the soul. [12]Conduct yourselves honorably among the Gentiles, so that, though they malign you as evildoers, they may see your honorable deeds and glorify God when he comes to judge.

1 PETER 2:1-12

Explanatory note

Notice how many metaphors are used in this passage—babies, stones, houses. The passage uses a lot of contrasting metaphors to build its message.

There are a lot of Old Testament allusions in this passage. You might like to look them up—see Psalm 34:8-14; Psalm 118:22; Isaiah 8:14-15; Isaiah 28:16; Isaiah 43:20-21; Exodus 19:6.

The words used for aliens and exiles imply people who have no home—this contrasts with the invitation to come to Christ who builds a spiritual home.

- Read the passage through once.
- Observe a few moments' silence.
- Read the passage a second time with different voices.
- Invite everyone to say aloud a word or phrase that strikes them.
- Read the passage a third time.
- Share together what this word or phrase might mean and what questions it raises.

Reflection   MARY GREGORY

Lord of the Church

For some this might be the most challenging part of the creed. For how can we believe that the Church is "one" when, in the words of Samuel J. Stone's famous hymn, it is "by schisms rent asunder, by heresies distressed"? Or how can we declare that the Church is "holy" when so much harm has been done in its name?

The answer might be to focus on God's creation of the Church, on God's sustaining of it, rather than on the way particular churches or individuals have distorted its identity.

In 1 Peter 2 it is clear that it is God's activity that is decisive for the Church: it is God who builds believers into a spiritual house (v. 5), God who gathers disparate individuals and makes them a people (v. 10), God who transforms them with God's mercy (v. 10).

It is primarily by God's grace that the Church is "one, holy, catholic, and apostolic," but in each generation the Church itself is called to live out that identity.

In celebrating and blessing a marriage, after the vows have been made and the rings exchanged, the priest stands before the couple and proclaims that they are "joined together" by God; the two are now newly joined to one another. This is also who they become as minute-by-minute, day-by-day they practice the sacrificial way of love and life set out for them in the vows.

It is God who builds believers into a spiritual house.

In the same way, through God's proclamation, the Church *is already* one, holy, catholic, and apostolic, a holy nation (1 Peter 2:9). Even so, the Church is to strive to live out this calling—to reflect its designation as "holy," for example by ridding itself of malice, guile, insincerity, envy, and slander (1 Peter 2:1). These two verses illustrate this paradox of the Church's identity: that it already *is* and is *becoming* holy—one, catholic, apostolic.

The Church is to strive to live out this calling.

In short
God has declared that the Church is already holy, but the Church is challenged to live out this calling and to work out what it means for its place and time.

For discussion

- What do you struggle with about the life of the Church in the present day? What do you rejoice in?
- Where do you see growth in unity, holiness, connectedness, and mission in the church you are part of today?

The marks of the Church

One—In the words of the catechism: "The Church is One, because it is one Body, under one Head, our Lord Jesus Christ."

In 1672 Sir Isaac Newton published a series of experiments where, by shining white light through a prism, he had demonstrated that it is made up of a spectrum of colors—of red, orange, yellow, green, blue, and violet. By refracting this rainbow through another prism, Newton found that it became white light once more.

The Christian Church is made up of a spectrum of churches.

Similarly, the Christian Church is made up of a spectrum of churches—each with their particular color or hue—which find their unity through the prism of the Trinity. Just as the persons of the Trinity form a single communion, so different expressions of life-together form one Church.

Holy—In the words of the catechism: "The Church is holy, because the Holy Spirit dwells in it, consecrates its members, and guides them to do God's work."

The creeds themselves were born out of a Church struggling to express its unity, to fight its way through controversy to a declaration of shared belief.

One of those controversies arose following the persecution of the Church by Emperor Diocletian when, in fear of their lives, some Christians sought to conceal their faith. In safer times these same Christians tried to rejoin the Church. A group called the Donatists refused to make them welcome, arguing that because they had denied their faith they were not worthy to be part of the Church. Augustine disagreed, pointing out that the Church is made up of sinners who have "received mercy" from God (1 Peter 2:10).

The holiness of the Church relies not on a community of people with impeccable moral judgement and flawless behavior but on the grace of God who counts them as righteous.

Catholic—In the words of the catechism: "The Church is catholic, because it proclaims the whole Faith to all people, to the end of time."

The Church is a foretaste of what God's kingdom will be like. In one of his parables about the kingdom (Luke 14:16-24), Jesus describes a banquet at which the invited guests fail to turn up and where, instead,

> *The host welcomes in people who, elsewhere, would be outcasts.*

the host welcomes in people who, elsewhere, would be outcasts: "the poor, the crippled, the blind, and the lame" (Luke 14:21).

Apostolic—In the words of the catechism: "The Church is apostolic, because it continues in the teaching and fellowship of the apostles and is sent to carry out Christ's mission to all people."

The Greek verb *apostellein* means to send forth—an apostle is one who is sent forth; a messenger.

The Church is apostolic in so far as it has received the message of the first apostles and in so far as it then passes on this message to others. Archbishop William Temple once said that "the Church is the only society on earth that exists for the benefits of its non-members"— the Church, then, must be a Church in mission, one continually going forth to pass on the faith it has received.

In short

The Church is called to be one in different expressions; declared holy by God; in all places, across all time and for all people (catholic) and sent forth with God's message for the world (apostolic).

For discussion

- What could your church do to express its God-given unity with other local churches, even those with whom you seem to share little common ground?

- How far is the church that you experience a place for all people? Are there ways it needs to change to become truly catholic?

- How much of the energy of your church is directed towards its non-members?

Journeying On

As this part of *Pilgrim* comes to an end, write on a piece of paper the most important lessons you will take away from the Bible readings, the reflections, the tradition, and your own experience of this group.

Share the two or three most important points on your list with the whole group in thanksgiving for God's grace.

Concluding Prayers

We believe in the Holy Spirit,
the Lord, the giver of life,
who proceeds from the Father and the Son.
With the Father and the Son he is worshiped and glorified.
He has spoken through the prophets.
We believe in one holy catholic and apostolic Church.
We acknowledge one baptism for the forgiveness of sins.
We look for the resurrection of the dead, and the life of the world to come. Amen.

As our Savior taught us, so we pray,
Our Father... (see p. 6)

Wisdom for the Journey

We are born in the womb of the church; we are nourished by her milk; and we are animated by her Spirit.

CYPRIAN OF CARTHAGE (*C.* 200–58)

The church is called catholic because it is spread throughout the whole world, from one end of the earth to the other, and because it teaches in its totality and without any omission every doctrine which ought to be brought to the knowledge of humankind, concerning things both that are seen and unseen, in heaven and on earth. It is also called catholic because it brings into religious obedience every sort of person, rulers and ruled, learned and simple.

CYRIL OF JERUSALEM (C. 315–86)

O God, make the door of this house wide enough
to receive all who need human love and fellowship;
narrow enough to shut out all envy, pride and strife.
Make its threshold smooth enough to be no stumbling-block to children, nor to straying feet,
but rugged and strong enough to turn back the tempter's power.
O God, make the door of this house the gateway to thine eternal kingdom.

THOMAS KEN (1637–1711)

The spiritually minded have tended to find the visible church a troubled and imperfect home. To found a "pure church" has long been the instinct of impatient zeal. But this instinct must be restrained. The visible church is to be borne with because it is the Spirit's purpose to provide a home of training and improvement for the imperfect. "Let both grow together until the harvest." The church is to be a mother, not a magistrate.

CHARLES GORE (1853–1932)

The body of Christ takes up space on earth. The incarnate Son of God needs not only ears or hearts, but living men and women who will follow him. That is why he called his disciples into a literal, bodily following. Having been called, they could no longer remain in obscurity, for they were the light that must shine, the city set on the hill which must be seen.

DIETRICH BONHOEFFER (1906–45)

What did I expect? That your people would be perfect? Did I forget the history and nature of man and what salvation is all about when I dreamed of a church free from misery, human ambitions, and failure?

PAUL GERES (1921–)

Notes

Introduction
You might want to look up 1 Corinthians 15:3-4, 1 Timothy 3:16 or Colossians 1:15-20.

Session One
Clement of Alexandria (*c*.140–*c*. 220), *Miscellanies* V, 11.
Gregory of Nyssa (*c*. 330–94), *Life of Moses*, 238.
C. S. Lewis (1898–1963), *The Great Divorce*, London, Geoffrey Bles, 1945.
Thomas Merton (1915–68), *No Man Is An Island*, New York, Harcourt, Brace & Co., 1955.

Session Two
Irenaeus (*c*. 130–*c*. 200), *Against The Heresies*, iv, 20, 6.
Julian of Norwich (1373–1417), *Revelations Of Divine Love*.
Justin (*c*. 100–165), *First Apology*, 2.
William Shakespeare (1564–1616), *Hamlet*, V, 2.

Session Three
Augustine (354–430), *Sermon 13 "On the Seasons."*
Bernard of Clairvaux (1090–1153), *Sermon 1 "On The Nativity,"* 2.
Geoffrey Studdert Kennedy (1883–1929), *The Hardest Part*, London, Hodder & Stoughton, 1918, 189.
Evelyn Underhill (1875–1941), *The Light of Christ*, London, Longmans, 1944.

Session Four
Augustine (354–430), *Sermon*, Guelfer 3.
Bernard of Clairvaux (1090–1153), *Sermon 1 "On the Epiphany,"* 1.
John Chrysostom (*c*. 347–407), *Homily "On the Burial Place and Cross,"* 2.
George Herbert (1593–1633), from "Easter."
Mother Julian of Norwich (1373–1417), *Revelations of Divine Love*, 22.
John Polkinghorne (1930–), *Belief in God in an Age of Science*, London, Yale, 1998.
Alexander Solzhenitsyn (1918–2008).

Session Five
Augustine (354–430), *Confessions*.
Basil the Great (*c*. 329–79), *On the Holy Spirit*, 9.
Richard Challoner (1691–1781), *Meditations*, "Whitsunday."
Isaac of Nineveh (seventh century), *The Ascetical Treatises*, 85.

Session Six
Dietrich Bonhoeffer (1906–45), *The Cost of Discipleship*, trans. R. H. Fuller, London, SCM Press, 1959, 223.
Cyril of Jerusalem (*c*. 315–86), *Catechetical Lectures*, 18.
Cyprian of Carthage (*c*. 200–58), *On the Unity of the Church*, 5.
Paul Geres, *Prayers for Impossible Days*, Philadelphia, PA, Fortress Press, 1976, 17.
Charles Gore (1853–1932), "The Holy Spirit and Inspiration," in *Lux Mundi*, ed. Gore, London, John Murray, 1889, 331.
Thomas Ken (1637–1711), *A Prayer Written for St Stephen's*, Wallbrook, London.